SORROW SOOTHERS:

MIND PLEASERS & VICTORY VERSES

KEDESHA DALLAS GOODE

Sorrow Soothers: Mind Pleasers & Victory Verses by Kedesha Dallas Goode

ISBN: 978-1-949343-48-9

Cover Design: Dionne R. Ramdeen
Book Design, Layout, Typesetting & Formatting: Dionne R. Ramdeen
Tel: (876) 339-2981
Email: dionnerachaelcreative@gmail.com
Website: https://dionnerachael.wixsite.com/creative
Interior stock images: https://pxhere.com

Revised Edition

First publication July 2017 by Krystal Cameron Designs Ltd.

Books may be purchased by contacting the author, Kedesha Dallas Goode,
at Kdallasgoode.com, kdallasgoode@gmail.com, @creativegoodenesshub, @kedgoode,
Facebook: Kedesha Dallas Goode, or online at amazon.com

Why Bother to Motivate?

FOREWORD

What is the reason for all of this? I cannot believe I asked myself this ridiculous question after having gone so deep into this project. This has been a burning desire for too long. How could I not? Know this; even the grown and mature thinkers slip into doubt and negativity. That is human! Which is exactly why I wrote this motivational book. Yes, firstly to add to the throng of uplifting stories out there, but more importantly, uplifting you, uplifts me; empowering you, empowers me; revamping you, revamps me; and renewing you, renews me. The world seems so impossible and confusing that sometimes neither you nor I know what's next. However, I can tell you that we need to be there for one another, for each other, that is, whoever your each other or one another may be. Look out for someone else, propose and promote positivity; neglect and deject negativity; embrace and face the reality that backward is not an option, but forward is the echoing decision. No man, no way, we cannot accept defeat. And so, I present this motivational book to you and to me so that we can jolt ourselves into elevating stories and poems that will add fruitfulness to the fruits we are struggling to grow within us and joy to the gems we are carving in our lives.

Let us be reminded that survival is the name of the game, struggles already claim its fame, and coming out on top is our aim in Jesus' name.

This revised edition would not have been possible without God's divine intervention and purpose. I dedicate this book to His glory!

Secondly, to My Parents, Siblings, Husband, and Daughter: each of you has added a unique element of learning and growth to my life, for which I am grateful.

THE CONTENTS OF MY HEART

The Underdog

The diamond in the rough,
The rose that inconspicuously blooms among the thorns,
Caught up in the multitude among them,
Solitude is your only friend,
Your victory you fight to defend,
Setting trends is not your means to an end,
You meditate over your story,
Your objective is to plot your way to gratifying glory,
No one knows for sure,
The way your life will go.
With life's fierce and raging winds,
Piercing beneath your skin,
Your patience then wears thin,
But with a faint, one-sided grin,
Your strong backbone overpowers your wishbone,
Very soon you realize you don't stand alone,
While He sits beside His father on the throne,
Defeat, weakness, pessimism, negativity
He ordains you not to condone,
So you stop and think, these wretched feelings and sentiments,
Do I then postpone?
No way, no how, they only spell detriments,
Kick them to the curb.

With them and your back against the wall,
Visualize your rise not your fall,
They think your chance of winning,
Is like a once bright light automatically dimming,
But you are the Underdog,
Shock society,
Shock yourself with empowered sobriety,
Clean sweep to your ultimate purpose,
Underdog, yes! kick up 'rumpus'
Roar renewed resilience,
Portray positive insistence,
Your collar tag, brags number one,
They thought you were over and done,
But in the end you've won!

As a child growing up, I felt like an underdog. I had dreams and aspirations of what I wanted to become, but I didn't have any motivation or a defined starting point. Most times I didn't know where to turn, didn't know where to look nor who to run to, but then I looked up and I found hope. And yes, many times I would still despair and doubt because my early life experiences seemed too much to bear. I was however, determined to make it, to push through the difficulties and achieve my goals.

Determination and faith in God built me; my drive for excellence propelled me. I know our journeys are different and our struggles even more, but never let your early setbacks, failures, or mistakes bankrupt what you can make a brighter tomorrow. With the right driving force and attitude, there must be a better way.

A Kaleidoscopic Beginning: Benign, Bold, Burdensome & Blissful

My childhood to adolescent into young adult life was fair to fine. My upbringing was economically unfortunate at times, but my penny-pinching challenges never hindered my dreams. I would always tell my friends "*I wasn't born rich, but I refuse to die poor.*" To me this simply meant working extremely hard, dabbling in my multiple passions, and always discovering new ways to advance myself, aim for the highest and never give up. I remember my mother being adamant about allowing me to participate in some kind of extra curricular activity whether it was at home, at school, or in the community. Back then, it didn't mean much. Sometimes it was fun, other times it seemed useless, but I look back now and think about how much these situations helped to build my character and personality.

Hmmmm … if I knew then what I know now!

Both my parents worked to provide for my siblings and myself. Back then, I realized that education and '*street smarts*' were the winning combination. It separates the go-getter from the complainer. I noticed that most persons had jobs in between jobs. My mother and father both had interesting '*hustling*' spirits, from owning a pharmacy, a mobile restaurant, wedding planner, car seller, to hairdresser, and many more. This was all to make an extra dollar as well as trying a hand at something new. I even caught on to the hustle. Back in High School and University I would comb colleagues hair, make sandwiches, and sell candy or chips. I knew then that dreaming was an opening to achieve the unattainable and welcome positive vibrations. I dreamt of doing well in school, completing university studies, and travelling the world. I tried my best to hold on to those dreams despite the hardships we faced. Nonetheless, I remember my parents were always trying, so I kept on trying too. Every summer I worked to get money, garner experience, and venture into unfamiliar territories. My

experiences ranged from working at a bank to assisting at a hair salon and coincidentally working at a primary school among many others. The work and school pattern were very useful and valuable. I cherish them more now than I did back then. The exposure certainly made me more eager to construct valuable goals and created a passion in me to persevere against all odds. The backdrop of my life was and still is painted with so many colourful experiences, both elevating and demanding. I went on a school trip to Cuba; my luggage abandoned me when they mistakenly went to another country, and I got them back about three weeks later. I remember being in Puerto Rico on a one-semester study program where I combed foreigners' hair to earn money. Also, while living in Spain and France, I taught English privately to learn more Spanish and French. These experiences among a myriad of others were very eye opening, exciting, adventurous and character testing. Today I am stronger, wiser, more aware and inexplicably grateful for all the lessons learnt. I wouldn't have wanted it any other way because I am a better me today. Today, I celebrate me: my learning experiences, my maturity, my accomplishments, my growth, my challenges, and my weaknesses. Everyday life teaches me something else and every twenty-four hours I have the luxury of being alive, I try to soak up more positive than negative. I have discovered that learning is a personal choice; once it becomes a priority and tenacity drives your actions, no one can stop your advancement. I salute learning; it is the cornerstone of success and failure because it is after all the trials and errors that you learn, grow and mature, which leans you closer to excellence.

Down to the Wire ... Mission Motivate & Inspire

Motivation and inspiration, whether intermittent or consistent, are necessary ingredients to: get over life's hurdles, help us exude our potential, and challenge us outside our comfort zone to achieve greatness. It is not in every circumstance that we feel a great urgency to push past pessimism and pain. However, after every setback, set yourself up to accomplish and conquer.

Life's dynamism is unpredictable, likewise our responses in those situations are unsure, so find value in the valleys of obstacles and challenges. Program your mind to prosper and only that! When you feel like you have fallen, prop up quickly to a thunderous rise. Push through the problems and press forward to your purpose. You are going to do it not because it's easy but because you can and you must.

On a Personal Note: The Work World and Onto Voluntary Teaching

In 2006 after graduating from the University of the West Indies (UWI), I was somewhat ready to take on adult life, that is; working, studying, working, more studying and simply that! A robotic sequence to improve my career because I just wanted more out of a mere B.A. in Spanish and International Relations with a taste of French. Finally, after what seemed to be a long wait – *May to September* – I gained full-time employment doing customer service duties. At first, it was new, challenging and took some amount of technique to master my tasks in order to be efficient and effective. However, as time progressed, I was hungry only for more – my Spanish acquisition that I sweated over for three years was nothing but a distant thought. There was a stall in my upward mobility because Spanish was not a part of the equation, but my insatiable lust for progress led me to the discovery of an institution that offered free Spanish classes to adults. *Voila!* I thought. That was the perfect opportunity to practice my Spanish, but intimidating also, as my main duty

was to teach basic Spanish to adults. Oh tot me! As I relished the thought, it became more real and then surreal. Might I mention, I offered to do it for free? Maybe not the best idea since my intention was to take on adult life, but my mom taught me: To achieve greatness, at some point you have to give of yourself – *sacrifice*; creep before you walk; '*kiss ass before you kick it.*' This advice definitely materialized as I am now kicking the classroom's butt, being very verse and passionate about my teaching profession, and of course, learning every day. At that interval in my life, I never got bored, neither of my 9-5 job nor of stepping into the unknown of teaching. I gained much more than I imagined. Sometimes it was hard because I had to mentally condition and prepare my mind to manage both job responsibilities and do it very well. My mind had to constantly govern my body to go above and beyond in an effort to be the best version of myself, as God would have it.

From Trouble Trance to a Victory Trajectory

Troubles, problems, trials, challenges, obstacles all share the common factor: they are inevitable. No one's life is problem free or liberated from troubles. They can bowl you over, knock you out, stunt your progress, stagnate your growth, and put you in a tumultuous trance. At times, when troubles are consistent, the proverbial phrase comes to mind: "*out of the fire, into the frying pan.*" What if you give in and give up; what if the anchor of your ship doesn't stay resilient; what if you glance to your left and to your right in comparison to others; what if you let go off your might to fight? Your road to recovery would be a very distant occurrence. Victory would be far-fetched. Turn a new leaf. You must go over and not under. Fight for your God given right to overcome. Carefully plot your trajectory path, only marked by victory. Get your mind right, get your speech in tact, channel your thoughts to climb - only to the top. *Painful or inconvenient, these same instances sharpen your priorities and add vim, vigour and vitality to your life's experiences.*

On a Personal Note: North Coast Experience

2007 Dawned! A New Year, but only almost a year into my '*adult life.*' By this time, I was searching for renewed progress. Teaching was rewarding, my other job became even more challenging, and yes I was going full speed ahead. Up to that point, the few persons I taught were impressed with my teaching content and style so much so that I gained more private classes. Good! Yay me! These opportunities were golden and helped honed my skills. Thirsty, motivated to move forward and eager to restart studying, I applied for a Master's Program in Spain to read for a degree in Sustainable Tourism. How far fetched! Not totally. I was off to a Spanish speaking country – *finalmente* – to eat, sleep and drink the language so much so that I could be very fluent and immerse myself into the culture. Nice objective but smooth sailing it certainly was not.

The trek to achieve this dream started with a very tedious scholarship application process, which I could not have done without the help of my teacher. After submitting my application, I began to mentally explore different ways to get myself ready for this next bold step. I found a type of internship in order to gain some work experience in an effort to be more marketable upon interview for the scholarship. I was blessed to get a job on the North Coast to be a Spa Manager at a very prominent hotel. Googoo, gaga! Hipee hoorah! I was flipping over, jumping up happy as I had to take massage classes. A new challenge, a fresh adventure, and I was also in charge of communicating with the Spanish guests. I was sad to leave teaching but ecstatic to have had the chance to still practice the language. The journey was unforgettable. I continued to learn valuable lessons of strength, self-motivation, a 'can do' anything attitude, and hunger to aim higher. Also, my entrepreneurial spirit led me to tackle many duties outside my parameters of responsibilities, one of which was to fill in for the cosmetologist in her absence. I did hair, nails and makeup. Funnily, I didn't know I had that in me but I was always willing to try because I relished the adventure of the unknown. Soon, I closed that chapter and eagerly got myself ready to start a new one.

Ponder Positivity, Think tenacity, Dare to Dream

"The happiness of your life depends on the quality of your thoughts." - Unknown

Feelings: whether negative or positive, embarrassing or uplifting, 'easy-breezy' or tedious, oblige us to do so many things. In the same way, we must adapt and adjust our persona to changes that come and go in our lives. No easy feat, but no way, no how can we allow ourselves to be defeated by feelings. The treacherous ones, those negative ones, even the ones that cast gloom and doubt over our responses to people and situations. When we can't fight those fierce feelings, what do we do? Sometimes it has to play out, other times we have to snap back with a positive attack, fight the maniac, to hell with this or that, I can't be bothered, why should I, God ye knows why, why me, what next, give up? Life can be described as a theatre production; whatever role you are given, play it to the best of your ability, shine through and claim the spotlight. Dream to become bigger and better so that you will be fulfilled and satisfied when you conquer and win.

On a Personal Note: Studies in Spain

As I prepared myself to take on the bold beginning of gaining a Master's Degree, my thoughts were on a mind-blowing roller coaster. I thought about the lengthy flight, the clothes I would wear on my first day, the thrill of living alone – being independent, people I would meet, shopping, new foods to eat, among other things, and barely the intensity of the academic program. I had no idea what was coming. There is something about stepping into the unknown that excites me, thrills me, and motivates me.

[You know what? The unknown can do so many things to you, both pleasing and plaguing of which you have to choose to promote and embrace the positive. When you hold on to the positive aspects of the unknown, its negative elements are mere lessons that add value to your growth].

The first day I arrived in Palma Mallorca, Spain, it was about 2am and I was already sunken and lethargic as my journey from Jamaica to the UK resulted in me being hospitalized as I unknowingly – to myself – passed out in the airport. So much for stepping into the unknown! I was still excited, roaring and ready to go. Fast forward to the first stages of settling in, yes! It was exceptionally hard; I mean living in the USA is somewhat different because there is a greater element of familiarity – language, people, etc. However, being far, far away from family, friends and my comfort zone was stifling at times because I just wanted a touch of familiarity to motivate me forward. I didn't have that so I had to depend on God to help me through every waking moment of my journey. Oh yea, He did! My faith skyrocketed to an unimaginable high. As I grew mentally and emotionally stronger I got physically stronger too. By that, I mean my Spanish got better. As a result, the cultural assimilation process was more seamless and comfort became my [growing] strong suit. I never imagined that being able to communicate would be so rewarding and fulfilling, that nothing else [lack of money and missing loved ones] seemed to matter. Studies were also very challenging, yes it was unmanageably hard because every single course was taught in Spanish. My weary eyes got somnolent from crying. Those tears saturated every fear, and this underdog became an overcomer, a dreamer, a believer, and in the end, an achiever. After the mountains and valleys, victories and venoms, struggles and strengths, positives and plagues, I finally earned my Master's Degree. WOW! I hoped for this, I prayed so hard for it, I earned it, and now I'm embracing it. Many events unfolded during the tenure of my graduate studies, many untold experiences, and an overflow of victories. I learnt so many valuable lessons, all of which are the pillars on which I cement myself to get through challenging times. I remember times when I had to print flyers advertising my services as a private tutor of English for native Spanish speakers. I liked this opportunity but it was a strategic tactic that would be mutually beneficial to both the student and myself. I would be indirectly learning Spanish while teaching English. It worked and I earned money too. I recall doing everything possible to get better at Spanish because I had a bigger picture in mind.

The Weary Walk Through Life and Then Some ...

Sick and tired, exhausted, fed up, 'pissed off', peeved, worn out, and just simply can't be bothered with work, people, your surroundings, your situations, yourself, your family or even your loved one. There comes that point in my life and your life when all emotional hell just breaks loose, leaving us just as dormant as a still life painting. There is that moment when you curl into your shell because you would rather not talk. That quiet moment when you just want everything and everyone to leave you and let you be free - free to dive into the dampness of your spirit. After you have soaked yourself in despair, there is always that opportune moment when someone comes along, something happens or a self-light bulb strikes and at that juncture you have no choice but to pick up the pieces, restructure and re-strategize to keep focused and go gain life's progress prize. For some persons, the tenure of this unwanted but inevitable moment will vary, but don't be bounded in the bind; walk out of misery's shoes and socks, jump out of problems' hole and take a full grip and control to add value to your valleys. Preach it. Practice it. Love it. Embrace it. And soon, you will be it!

On a Personal Note: The Job Hunt

In 2009, I came home from two years of intense, amazing and eye-opening experiences in Spain with bittersweet emotions. On the one hand I was excited to come back to my roots and on the other hand I was in a nostalgic trance wishing to be in Mallorca, Spain. Nevertheless, I was ready for the world of work, ready to make some money, ready to take the professional world by storm and ready to officially start a new phase of my life. I remember being in Spain and praying for many things, one of which was to get multiple jobs so that I would not be solely dependent on my parents. Faith would have it that I worked at the Venezuelan Institute part time, the University of the West Indies, and at least three private tutoring classes. These experiences were very useful,

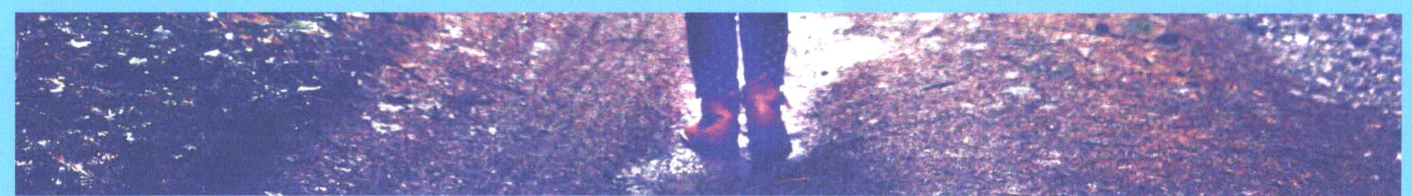

my teaching skills grew to an expert level, and it is still growing. At this point of my life, I was on a professional high. The constant teaching kept my mind occupied, my craft sharpened, and my passion propelled to embrace the bigger things to come. Soon, I got a full-time teaching job at a private school; I was the High School Spanish teacher. As tough as getting the job was, I rose to the occasion and gave this position my all. Speaking of an awkward acquisition; when I learnt about this job, I envisioned myself being in the position before officially being chosen, until I wasn't chosen. I was torn, because after doing the interview and receiving very affirmative feedback, I soon found out that one of my Venezuelan colleagues from my part-time gig got the job. When he conveyed his excitement and thrill, I was shocked, dumbstruck and confused but at the same time happy for him. Hey! I am human, I felt extremely sad because the compass seemed like it was pointing right in my direction, but it veered off my radar. After a bawl brawl with my mom, she reassured me that nothing good comes easy; you have to sweat for it, work hard for it until it's your time to get it. Then you would have earned it. Boy! I did earn it after what seemed like a long mental toil. One day, I got a call saying that I should come in to sign a contract for the position of Spanish Teacher. God really worked and still works in mysterious ways. Truthfully, this experience taught me that anything, I mean anything that is destined to be yours will definitely be yours. It's neither your time nor anyone else's. Instead, it's God's timing. You don't get what you want when you want, but you do get what you need when it's good for you. The experience I garnered from the position really elevated my craft as a teacher and refined my skills to learn more so that I could impart knowledge effectively. Iremember being really weary because a lot of challenges came at me. So many that I felt as if my only option was to give up, but my previous travel experiences thickened my skin. My mother also taught me to shine through every single situation more so the 'bad' ones because your verbal and physical responses are what matters most. Having the right response or bouncing back quickly after a downfall really enriched my maturity and added so much value to mycharacter. I learnt that bad times are hard, but torturous times are even worse when you cannot see the big picture. It depicts that strength of character is like a life jacket that saves you from any drowning situation.

An Unchanged Past, Fuelled by an Untamed Future

Here's the analogy: the bliss and serenity of the beach has a calming feeling that attracts everyone. The sand is an element of the beach that we cannot escape even after beach day is done and over. Do the remnants of the sand stay hidden behind your ears, tucked between your toes, or snuggled under your fingernails? That's the past! Even when you clean it from your physical self, some bits of it still linger with you. So, how do you proceed? The residual sand symbolic of fun certainly does not hinder your normal routine, in the same way any scenario the past paints should not push you backward. **P.a.s.t: P**ersevere **a**midst the **s**truggles and **t**urmoil; and, **P**ush **a**long with **s**trength and **t**enacity.

On a Personal Note: Embrace Change

From 2009 to 2012, I was busily entangled in 'adult life.' Work was so tastefully motivating that I went back to school in order to solidify my qualifications as a teacher. My Bachelor and Masters Degrees were noteworthy, but to be very marketable as a teacher I needed a Post Graduate Diploma. I did the Diploma in Education with a focus on Foreign Language Teaching for all levels: primary, secondary, and tertiary. This added another progressive element to my qualifications that afforded me the opportunity to get a consistent part-time job with the University of Technology and the University College of the Caribbean. I was an Adjunct Lecturer teaching both online and face-to-face Spanish. What growth! I had to embrace the changes in my life in order to achieve more than I ever thought possible. I was absolutely gratified because I learnt so much while still eager to learn more and be more. I also did weekend classes to re-oil my rusty French that would be an even greater asset to me in the long run. My thirties seemed like a stone throw away. As a result, I soon discovered another career prospect to step into an unfamiliar territory and embrace change; I applied to teach for a year in France, and I was successful. Whoopie dee! Immersion! France! I was flabbergasted! How could I not take advantage of

this experience to improve my French, maybe teach it upon return to Jamaica, and advance my career? Even though I was woven into a steady routine for a couple of years, I was not afraid to embrace change.

[Do not be afraid. I repeat, don't you ever be afraid to embrace change. While routine represents stability, change is a necessary ingredient that creates a balance pattern that rewards you in indescribable ways. Change creates more experiences that build you brick by brick. It broadens your horizons and enables ample maturity as well as stamina that will cultivate and encourage solid individual development. Don't run from it because you can learn from it].

As is customary, my life is not A-Z. There is always some challenge, hiccup, obstacle or lesson. I always tried not to let any unpleasant past experiences or encounters [of which I had many] curtail my courage or dampen my strong will to overcome. I was a veteran of newness, unafraid of the unknown. Yeah right! I was still tested and many unpredictable situations tried to bold me over, but I was strong. I prayed every day, held on to my faith, learnt to depend on God even more, and I pressed forward. Notably, my mother was a tower of strength that kept me grounded and motivated. Being the person that I am, I could not just teach, I also did private tutoring and went to classes to advance my French knowledge. Teaching in France at the primary and secondary levels allowed me to experience an aspect of the French culture that enabled me to assimilate very quickly. I thoroughly enjoyed it. My mentors were useful and awesome guides for me. I made many pleasant memories; I learnt uncountable lessons that were rich in growth and maturity. I travelled around Europe and quenched my thirst for adventure, change, and wisdom. I was ready to go home to welcome the new path of my life and career.

Excite & Ignite! I Can See Success' Flickering Lights

Jamaicans would say, '*mi glad suh til mi glad bag buss.*' Good news can be such pleasant music to the ears. Happiness can be so extreme that its effect just electrifies and shines such a bright blinding light in any undesirable circumstance. An accomplishment, an objective fulfilled, a fear conquered, an exhaled sigh of relief, an ear to ear grin, a warm heart, an uplifted spirit are all moments when being happy cannot be undermined by misery's mayhem. And yes, you and I should be happy; we are indeed deserving of that '*tickle me fancy*' happy feeling. It is often said that the happiness is looking beyond life's imperfections and basking in the possibilities of what you can make it. Truthfully, as humans, we sometimes struggle mentally to be in a consistent mode of good cheer and great joy. Simply, snowball the best things of your life and the situations while filtering the dreadful dregs of fear, worries and disappointment, intend to win, insist to be at peace and strive to make yourself happy, irrespective of. For sanity's sake do it, do it, and don't stop doing it.

On a Personal Note: Full Circle – Tutor, Teacher, Lecturer, Mother & Wife

In 2013, I returned home from my teaching/school stint in France jobless, but swell with growth and experience. I recall that in 2008 I used to dress up as if I had a job and went to business seminars or AGMs to distribute my business cards in an effort to make connections and market myself. Being jobless, I was back at this effective procedure. I sent out resumes and unexpectedly popped up at business places with a resume and an application letter in hand to persistently leave a mark with the hopes of getting a job. My persistence returned me to work at the University of Technology and University of the West Indies. This time I taught both Spanish and French. I was humbled and absolutely grateful. My desire came to fruition! My prayers were answered! God

strategically prepared me for this. I was so ready! In all of this, I managed the marketing and public relations for a corporate company and I also started another passion – graphic designing. Yet again, I was on a professional high, my career was growing and my teaching came full circle.

I was pleasantly surprised when I was re-offered a position as Spanish and French teacher at my previous teaching job working with High School students. At this point, I resumed full time teaching and lecturing while adding French to my pedagogical portfolio. God's timing was unimaginable and truly uplifting. I was a *workaholic* who drowned myself into work so that I could soak up all the experience necessary to continue improving my craft, learn new things, and grow. Then, that time came; the unexpected yet welcoming responsibilities of motherhood and marriage were pleasantly laid at my feet. I stepped on the figurative mat and happily slid into these demanding yet rewarding roles. Suffice to say, these new hats I've been wearing have served me some hot meals of challenges, some cold ones of setbacks and numerous delicious ones of triumphs and accomplishments. I have learnt a lot about myself including the reservoir of talent and potential that I have, to do more than what meets the eye. Being a mother and a wife never slowed me down. I was still motivated to operate as if I were an octopus trying to tackle many things. I still lectured part-time at the University of Technology, did some wedding jobs, continued various private classes and sold jewelry. There are many more passions in the making. Present day, I am fervently working towards unlocking and tapping into my *purpose-s*.

Fulfill Your Purpose ... On Purpose

Made up mind + Passion Pursuits - Negative Nuances = Purpose Fulfilled. On Purpose

Pursuing your purpose is the end result of the equation, but where does it begin? What excites you? What passionate thoughts permeate your mind? Anything, Something … Think! Think! Think … Nothing?

Finding your purpose can sometimes be so daunting and pointless to a mind that's overcome with challenges, overwhelmed with despair, and simply crumbled by disappointments. There has to be something. You can find it. You must find it in order to operate your life in a positive and uplifting way. Positive energy and optimistic thoughts aren't naturally engrained, not with the upsurge of problems that stick to us like parasites. Each person's primary purpose is to make up his or her mind, YES! Condition and/or train your thoughts to think positive, hope for goodness, and don't stop doing it. Do it for the good of your personal progress; do it for the benefit of a sane mind, one that will function at its optimal capacity.

On a Personal Note: Full Circle – What's Next? Finding More, Doing the Most …

[Tapping into your purpose is so important that it is the driving force behind self-fulfillment as well as self-actualization that will elevate your levels of achievement and happiness to incredible highs. Once you dig deep and desire assiduously to discover your purpose and strategically work towards executing it, you would have eliminated a lot of tyranny and annoyance that comes of leading an aimless life].

It is as if my mind is constantly in overdrive mode. Thinking about what? I am always pondering on a myriad of things; a business venture, planning ahead, figuring out something new to engage

myself in or strategizing to accomplish a goal. This is one of my ways of truly discovering what my passion is, and simultaneously my purpose will weave itself into the web of pursuit and progress. I have always had a burning desire to uplift people by listening to them, motivating them and cheering them on in their happiness and successes. This indirectly empowers me in a very comforting way. Somehow, teaching has given me that opportunity but not totally, and so I have committed to this, writing – one of my biggest and most humbling projects that has been a long-standing passion that I know will catapult me into my ultimate purpose. This medium of sharing has given me a renewed spirit to wake up, shake up, and shine through every single thing – good or bad. I have witnessed and still see how God has plotted my life's path to achieve my goals. My daily tasks, I try to: open my eyes, seize opportunities, trust the process, push past pessimism, learn from setbacks and meekly make my way to victory.

Let Go ... Loose free ... Liberated

Ever been on a zipline? Me, no! Other persons, maybe so. Ever been on a roller coaster?

Me, Yes! For other persons, it's the best. Both activities do not allow 100% individual control. It's more like 70-30. For control freaks this is ludicrous, for adventurers, this is sheer bliss.

Do you have overly obsessive controlling disorder? Or, Do you ride with the rewards of risk taking?

I concur, the two main types of characters are the control monsters also known as *tame 'n' lame* and the risk takers otherwise known as the *rule breakers*.

For the control addicts, having absolute and total control over almost everything empowers them, soothes them and functions better for them. They can't choose any other way to operate. Letting go, is a resounding no, no. They micro manage everything blow by blow. When they do this, what is the ripple effect? Nothing, they say, everything is circumspect! On the other hand, the adventurers find comfort in the thought of going where the wind carries them; they most times go 'on a wing and a prayer.' They are always willing to take risks, challenge themselves, and step out of their natural habitat of operating to just simply *letting go*.

Let go of PROBLEMS:

The first order of business is to drop problems right at your feet and allow God to navigate your way. You cannot possibly fix everything or most things; you will be MAD. Problems play a major part in everyone's life. NO ONE, I repeat, NOT ONE PERSON is free from or unknowing of problems. How you tackle them and choose to overcome them is the key to mental liberation and to curb your intolerable frustration. If you need a fortified army of cheerleaders to take you through, well, choose them carefully, cherish them and reciprocate with them. If you need to train your mind every day to push through, do just that, push pass the parasite of problems. I know it's a mental thug and pull of your mind/thoughts and actions. But we have to prioritize our thoughts so that we can filter the things or aspects of life that will motivate us forward and put us in a better mental space. It's a work in progress that desires propel and actions solidify.

Let go of PEOPLE:

Covetousness is the babble on everyone's lips. Most times people just always feel like someone for some reason or another is 'jealous' of or 'bad mind' them for something. Fact is: we all wish to be like someone else or have something that they have, BUT what you do with that wish is the telling part. Think about a motivational book or even a story, one that adds vigour to your vitality, hope to your hopeful and reality to your dreams. Don't you wish to become and think like the advice of the motivator? For sure! Therefore, channel your thoughts and actions in an upward direction or else when negativity consumes you, that plague haunts you, demonizes you and confuses you. TAKE CONTROL, Let go of people and make positivity a priority. If someone is not moving to your beat, catapulting you forward or riding on high positive waves of life, simply let go, leave him or her be. Know what you want, who you want to be, champion your cause, captain your ship, pilot your plane, and believe that you can do exceeding abundantly above what you are able to ask or think, because GOD granted us that. We need to quietly but fervently search to find it and control it to produce purity of life.

Let go of WORK:

The authors of *'Rich Dad, Poor Dad'* and *'The Seven Day Weekend'* denounce the orthodox way of work. The former author dismisses the idea of the nine to five regimens and upholds true professional happiness and comfort that is achieved by means of entrepreneurial pursuits. The latter author encourages a carefree nine to five routine that allows employees the liberty to work on their own terms while getting the job done. Which would you rather? Maybe none, maybe one, or a little of some. Absolute gratification will never be achieved neither by working for yourself nor someone else. We as people are hardly ever satisfied. We always want more. Our idea of the perfect professional situation is far reaching to the bare eye or a simple mind. Work is, for the most part what we make it. Which is why each person has to answer these questions as an individual in order to let go of the discomfort caused by work. What are you wiling to work with (tolerate) versus what are you willing to walk away from (give up)? Most of us work with or tolerate our jobs for the money, for complacency sake, because of fear or lack of opportunity among a number of other things. While some of us walk away from it because of career growth, courage, frustration, or despair. Whatever your situation is, find the courage to let go. When you carefully figure out what hurdles you will hop over and the battles you are willing to fight you will automatically move to a level of maturity that will cause you to strategize in order to minimize. If you are unhappy at work let go of what is, have a plan, and hold on to it. Devise a strategy to recognize, understand and release the anger, which will eventually minimize the distress of work. Really and truly let go! If you don't, you will be miserable as an individual, misguided in your actions, misinformed of opportunities and meager with positive energy. This is very hard considering the extremities of the problems and challenges in the work world, but what is the other option? Definitely not to give up! Let go! Negativity is a no no. Whether you work for someone, yes or no. Allow good things to flow.

Let go of PRIDE:

Amplified pride punishes progress and pushes people farther apart. Pride is such an engrained plague inside of us. Have you ever felt it inside you? There are certain characteristics that you nurture and there are others you blatantly deject. Pride is definitely one to let go. It ruins the way we interact with people, it measures others unfairly, it focuses on failure and it stifles humility. Let go of Pride. This is one trait of being human that you want to dismiss and do away with. Let go of Pride. It eats away everything good you have, leaving you with nothing. It's not worth it in the end. Say sorry if you must, right a wrong because it is just. Let go of Pride. The problematic predicament of pride masks mistakes, prolongs ego and focuses on what is beneath and not above. Let go of Pride. This is an ongoing reminder for you and me, so that mentally and emotionally we can work towards being free. Free from the clutter of pride and free to be better, do better and live better. As pride free as can be.

Making a Difference

As I solemnly sit,
I rumble through my heart.
I find scars, hurt, pain,
I rumage deeper,
I discover happiness,
That 'gota de felicidad',
That stains the heart,
It doesn't depart,
For it plays an important part,
That makes it all worthwhile.
Worth it to live,
Worth it to strive,
Causing me to dive and heap together,
All the 'pedazitos' of happiness,
Creating a collage,
One that will give me a renewed heart,
A new spirit,
A new attitude,
A new mood,

So long pessimism,
Goodbye anger,
Take your flight pain,
Au revoir suffering,
Get comfortable Miss positivity,
Master take charge,
All the more faster,
Fostering change,
Embracing hope,
Come walk with me,
Beloved peace,
Precious joy and cherished happiness,
Let's make it official,
Our love affair,
For it I'll hold dear,
To my heart,
With no intention to part,
Come hug me,
As I venture into the unknown.

gota de felicidad- drop of happiness & pedazitos- little pieces

Strength

Boxed about, spat upon,
And challenged beyond reasoning,
The two-footed scoundrels try,
They themselves don't even know why,
Why?
Why they rape the 'I' of my inner strength,
My poor heart laments for,
The character that has been the foundation,
Of my accreditation,
But with self motivation,
I hug that thing called strength,
Hide it in the hallow palm of my hands,
Protecting it, preserving it,
Because they are not deserving of it,
After it all I will rise, soar above the skies,
Being forever wise,
I stand tall and open my eyes.

Affairs of the Heart

Boom, boom, boom …
It beats tirelessly,
Room, room …
It roars unassumingly,
Why? What's wrong?
From the start, the heart cannot part,
Part ways with feelings of despair,
For which there's no repair,
Love! Showered from above,
Fear! What a scare?
That piece of peace I don't want to cease,
Affairs of the heart …
Torn, tattered, crumbled,
That's the state of the heart.
The heart … ah holla, bawl,
It wants to find a way,
But feelings cause it to stray,
Stray from a positive pathway,
I pray, feelings prey,
I pray, feelings stay,
I pray, feelings come and go away,
There has to be another way …

Change

The wind rushes towards her,
Her eyelids flutter catching back its vision,
But all too quick.
The rushing wind takes a grip,
Controlling everything,
Remixing the little elements of her being,
Her environment that stood in its place.
Right before her face,
It came dashing like A 100 metre race.
Change, she thought, like the brisk wind,
It transforms everything.
Like seasonal fruits,
So all other things has its roots,
One that may or may not change in an instant,
She had to rearrange to accommodate …
Change,
Change her talk, switch up her walk,
Change her stance and take her mark,
Ready to start,
She's ready to embark,
On that journey,
Yes, sometimes it will get blurry,
But her eagle eyes were focused on the
Accolade,
Be wise, she advise,
This is your moment,
Your time to accept change,
Resurrect yourself and adjust to change.

Sweetest Victories

Hmmnn...Childhood to adolescence, the extreme pleasures of the unknown, ah fun times for we're not yet grown, still we condone the riskiness of just simply keeping abreast with the trivialities minus difficulties.

Frolic, laughter, adventures, memories of stories untold, how quickly they unfold and in an instant we grow old, old to embrace adulthood at which time we dig deeper and deeper for purpose, meaning, objective ...

BUT TAP!

We then become selective, *stoshush*, defensive, pensive, reflective because adulthood becomes our solitude where we take a step back and now try to put our lives on track, but before we know it *ah* million and one challenges attack ...

Persevere without fear! Tenacity, grab it up with audacity, *nuh bada wid* passivity, *ah* more *livity* should be the daily activity... *chat bout* negativity, it *nuh* got *nuh damn* place. For this race is indeed for those who can endure cause the obstacles *dem* come even more *an* more but for sure, *wi* back broad to *di* core cause at the end of the multiple rise *an* fall, we creep, we crawl, *wid* our back against the wall an all *ah bawl* but watch *yah* now *nuh* still we toil, oh what a fright! Cause one day, one night after all, the sweetest victories WILL come to one *an* all.

Many times our comfort zone holds us captive so much that a glimpse of the unknown unknown leaves us feeling alone. We can not condone operating in the unknown because we think outside our 'home' is a dangerous zone. Sometimes we step back into our comfortable routines without exploring to broaden our horizons and take leaps into new territories so that we can grow and progress. I challenge us to do something we have never done before to get to somewhere we have always dreamed of.

Faith with Wings

Like a bird, oh how I wish to command the
Sky …
Soar away, far, far away to a place that is
Higher than I …
Where no one can tell me where, or when,
Not even why …
Like an eagle oh how I wish to seamlessly,
Unmistakably swoop down,
To capture prey with pinpoint accuracy …
Realities won't get a chance to attack me,
With its bare face audacity …
Land and water lifestyles,
They drive me wild …
So much sometimes I have to
Bawl and cry …
Pessimism and trials eavesdrop and pry …
The defensive reply of optimism and tenacity,
Sometimes can't even get a bligh …
And you wonder why I want to fly …
Up there in the sky,
My wings are spread wide …
My eyes on the prize,
It is there I rise,
With power to conquer my fears,
Freedom to let go my tears,
Transcendence to exercise my resilience,
I am content now,

I take a bow,
What a joy faith with wings, brings.
Free I fly with ease and just as I please,
Through the breeze,
I meander through the sighing trees.
Truth is, earth is my home,
And I as I continue to roam,
Through the adventures of life I often moan,
And groan,
But I know I am NOT alone …
Like the bold peacock,
I restock, positivity to my foundation,
And I, yes I, step with prowess towards
Progress.

As I scribbled my inner thoughts, I know that we go through so much sometimes that only faith and prayer will exonerate us. Sometimes we wish for a permanent end to our problems and challenges. Well, we have to maintain our sanity. Never despair my friend. The Father is always near even when you are not lending a listening ear. Just be prepared when He kicks your blessings into full gear. Motivation for us! Faith as small as a mustard seed can move mountains. Be strong. Stay positive. Better must come.

A Brighter Day

Deep down in problems' hole,
Over pessimism she seems to have no control,
She's told about this notion of,
A brighter day,
She has no emotion of,
For her, there's no better way.
Challenges, obstacles, hurdles,
Blind her progress,
Leading her a stray,
Regress, regress, regress,
It's non-stop stress …
In spite of it all little does she know,
She is still blessed.
Through the pain is the only way she will grow,
A brighter day will come!
She reiterates to the problem called – foe,
Slowly but surely she is convinced to:
Practice positive emotions,
Play with uplifting vibrations,
Create within her an inner sensation,
To overcome,
To get up and stand up,
Wake up and shake up,
Stand strong,
Woman up and free up,
Fill her life's cup with,
If not all but most of,
The progressive and
Positive juices,

To boost her seduces,
Her seduction,
That of ultimate deduction,
Deduct stress and pain,
Fight through problems and struggles'
Pouring rain,
After all she now knows she will gain,
A brighter Day,
No complain!

We are so deep down in the belly of life's problems and obstacles that sometimes our heads can't even look up to notice that the dark days CANNOT and WILL NOT last forever. But if only we can find some way to be determined, focused and hopeful enough to fight back and trust God to take us through. There is indeed a time for everything under the sun, and the time of storms and war in your life is only a speed bump that should not and ought not to cause a permanent clump in your progressive state of mind and being. Speak life into the lifeless situations and command them to hold their place while you continue firmly and steadily in the race of life. Life is what we make it. I am learning every day in every way to make it better and better and better even when 'life' presents itself as bitter. Inner strength and Peace with God!

The Journey

Imagine yourself at the top of the road,
Looking toward, looking forward,
To bear the heavy loads, loads of:
Challenges & obstacles,
Broken dreams & insurmountable troubles.
Imagine yourself fulfilled after the
Mountains & moe hills,
Revamped & rejuvenated,
After being dished some of life's
Inevitable 'pot *scrappins*',
You cry and cry,
You wonder why oh why,
Why do these problems
Never seem to be shy.
You're bolstered with reality's bold reply:
The journey is not a sudden achievement,
The journey is not a quick race,
The journey is a ment, a 'made up'
Ment-ality
Not one you can start & erase.
The journey is about:

Preparation to endure,
Through the tidal waves that will infiltrate
Your shore.
Faith in God to believe,
Even when you cannot clearly perceive.
Motivation to stay strong,
Even after all your strength is long gone.
Determination to fulfill your objective,
Even when being a detective
To their ulterior motive.
Knowledge of your atmosphere,
Even after life's scary scares,
Do you dare?
To possess that rare characteristic,
To bear life's terrible tactic,
Even after the dramatic static.
The journey will take you through
All of this,
But remember this,
In the midst of all of this,
God's grace is the most pleasant bliss.

The Riveting Rise & Forceful Falls

Heading forward to my riveting rise,
Stretched out to claim my prize,
To gain what is rightfully mine,
Whilst I envision my steady rise,
The warning amber lights didn't startle me,
Because. Still I rise.
Toiling tenaciously to the top,
Until, to my dismay,
The red lights of their mischief and mind,
Games brought me to a halting STOP.
They startled me,
I gave up on rising to the top,
Their uncanny ways and filthy craze,
Craze, crazy about my fall.
Spread out like an eagle,
Nowhere to fly, as tears filled my eyes,
I'm left to bawl, bawl, bawl,
As the surmounting defeat turns into …
Into a boisterous brawl,
I'm unwillingly backed up against that wall.
They never saw plan B,
Coming, coming, coming,
Towards me as I stood tall,
Grab it, control it & own it,
Still I rise after the fall,

Failure? I dethrone it,
Foe?
They build my backbone brick by brick,
My threshold now thick,
Like an inflated balloon,
Their attempts to prick,
To prick and stick,
Getting numerous kicks when I fall,
Fall flat on my face,
But with style and grace,
I jump,
I rise after the forceful falls and
Finish my race,
Because I can endure,
While they are swift and brave
My stamina kept me going,
For more and more.
Their haste and distaste cripple them,
From their waist to their baseless base,
Only mouth left,
Nothing to say now,
But to clap and give Me a bow
Kapoom Pow … I made it …
Look at me Now!

Beat Yourself Up ...

Many times you're wrong,
Sometimes you're right,
Even if you put up a fight,
You can't hide from the bright light,
The glare that stares you in the eye,
You're scared now,
Instead of being lifted high,
It hits you with the reply – "you're a failure,
You can't make it, step back *nuh badda* try",
Now what? Beat yourself up and cry,
Oh really! But why?
You mean you not gonna try? Give up,
Back down, now you're shattered and torn;
Overwhelmed and worn …
Get up, jump up, you say you're resilient,
But you can't forget, troubles are consistent,
But yes persistent you are to
"Fake it 'til you make it" at least so they say,
Come on now …
Don't stray from the realness of reality,
With alacrity, push through,
And maintain your sanity,
Dem tings yah nuh worth *yuh* mental stability,
But *cho, nuh* beat yourself up,
Free yourself up,
Stamina'rize' your thoughts, to be …

Bold: grab and hold your dreams,
Strong enough: to right your wrongs,
Determined: to focus even when caught up
In the whirlwind,
Beat yourself up, because of failure,
Regrets, defeat …
Remember …
Life goes on, grab a treat,
Stand to your feet,
No retreat, no surrender,
Victory we'll proclaim when we meet and
Greet in December …

As I penned my thoughts, our lives continue to unfold with its unpredictable events and situations going from hot to cold. When you feel like beating yourself up, please remember there's something better waiting on the other side. Keep climbing, pushing and peaking at your objectives. Find enrichment from everything, whether good or bad. Booster words of encouragement for you and me, from me to you. God allows adversity not to break us, but to make us better. Live strong. Live clean. Live as One.

The Long Wait in Patience

They that wait upon the Lord shall renew their strength; they shall mount up with wings as eagles; they shall run, and not be weary; and they shall walk, and not faint. - Isaiah 40:31

W.A.I.T – *w*ondering *a*nxiously *if* *t*hat *t*ime
Will come.
Tick tock goes the clock,
Your body now numb,
You try to suppress your shock,
As you question if that time will ever come.
You wait and wait and wait,
Stalemate, long outdate,
Now frustrate …. Overtake and,
Demotivate the wait.
But Faith, says,
Wait and be of good courage,
Or is it fate? That dictates,
Take it for what it is, and,
Date the wait.
Many things may be at stake,
Dreams that you already make,
Mistakes you want to unmake.
Hurdles to leap,
Barriers to break,
Obstacles to shake,
Give or take, you still must wait.
Wait allows you to:
*W*ork *a*ssiduously, *i*ncessantly *t*owards
Your dreams.
By this time your desire screams,
Your objective gleams,
And your long patience beams,
Alas! Patience wins,
Victory grins,
Results!
You achieved it. You got it.
You earned it.
Indeed you waited for it!

Blank Thought Tank

Life comes full circle when you understand
Its simplicity, its complexity, its diversity.
Life comes alive when you dare
To persevere,
Life gives you a full range of worries
And fear,
Life is unpredictable when dear hearts,
Become mere darts,
Darts aimed at your heart - sudden death,
Its threat - wreck, resurrect, interject …
Perplex!
What the heck!
And then …
Life provides memories to treasure,
Memories beyond measure,
Ones to have and hold,
Ones that dreams and aspirations
Are yet to behold,

But life can be so bitter, so cold,
I declare – to stand bold.
Bold, Bold, Bold, Bold, Bold,
Be bold she's told,
Damn it! This fake it 'til you make it idea,
Is getting old.
Cold, Crude realities are parasitic,
I am frantic,
The semantic-S, have no logic.
So what, the eulogy I live to write,
Will be tragic,
This is a democrat, I can be democratic!
The power is vested in me,
To be,
Mentally free, shine with glee
Behold what I see,
Conquer and cure from deep within me.

The Physical "I"

The innocent eyes of babies behold purity,
Their sporadic or incessant cries,
Deviate the norms of calamity,
And in the midst of it you struggle,
To maintain your sanity,
Your weary eyes have already beheld,
The world's fierce audacity.
Your short-term vision has distorted,
Your long-term decision,
Problems and woes come at you,
Like life threatening incisions,
Survival or Suicide,
What's your mission?
Achievement and success,
Is beyond your eye sight,
You have every right to grab it,
With all your might,
Catch the visionary flight,
What you see is what you get?
Neglect and fret,
Over life's negative threats,

I, can't be bothered,
I, am tired of trying,
I, numb 'til,
I, not even crying
I, am so soaked with it all,
I, am choked, guaranteed to fall,
I, am a failure,
I, am not good enough,
I've had enough,
It's rough, rough, rough.
Me, myself and I,
After all is said and done,
Me, myself and I …
I! have won,
I! have overcome,
I! have lost some,
But I,
I! will accomplish much more than one,
It begins with – I
It ends with – I
I, I, I, I,
Me, myself and I.

The Power of Obedience; Its Reflection of God's Faithfulness & Truth: *My Testimony*

As I sit to pen this chapter of the book's revised version, I must echo the scripture, "Great is" indeed "Thy faithfulness." I stand on the truth as a living example that if you "wait on the Lord, and be of good courage He will strengthen thy heart." My eyes are overcome with tears of joy and happiness because my year's journey has mirrored the affirmation which proclaims, "whatsoever things you pray for, believing, you will receive." The latter scripture does not imply that God's will be neglected. However, it assures that His timing and His way to fulfill our desires must align with the blueprint He has for our lives. When I think about my various passions and my zeal to do more, be more and achieve more, I often get caught up in my way. I have come to realize that when you pray earnestly, put God first place and do your part, He materializes your dreams mightily for His glory. The scripture holds true, "His ways are higher than my ways and His thoughts are higher than my thoughts." So, I learnt how to pray, listen, listen some more, be patient and act wisely. This is a snippet of my testimony.

In 2017, I was at a point in my life where my mainstream employment was wearing me thin – my creative juices were depleted to dregs. I felt unfulfilled, down, and incomplete. I knew I wanted more, so I was eager to know what God had in store. I pushed myself beyond my comfort zone; I persevered so much that I secured some opportunities that I hungered for. I wanted one of them to materialize, but nothing! While on the brink of a breakthrough (as I thought) nothing came through. I was still 'stuck' in the rut of my job. As my tenacious self would have it, I pressed God by praying, fasting and focusing on the message in what seemed like a mess. In the midst of this journey I became weary, distracted, discouraged and sometimes sad. When those emotions arose, I sunk in it, but I quickly rose and pushed some more. The times when I felt defeated the most, I prayed even more; I sought God's direction for sure because I was resolute to make it. I knew from previous experiences that delay does not mean denial. God has done too much for me to doubt Him. But wow! It's not easy to wait for something that you want so badly. No one would ever fully know my plight because I believe that integrity and excellence means do what you have to do to the best of your ability until you can do what you want to do with freedom and peace. My gateway to personal upliftment and peace came with the birth of *Empowerment Conversations*©. This initiative that was ordained by God, it was

my sustainer, my anchor and my cushion in the midst of doubt and fear. Each month's message inspired me, and more importantly, liked writing them.. Fast forward to the current year 2018; I became stronger, more enlightened, fervent in my faith and consistent with my prayers. After many questions to God, I came into the realization of His instructions to me, and I responded with obedience. I was definitely scared, but I gained the strength and did it. I quit my job! I took a leap of faith and sacrificed it all by following God's direction and guidance. My husband was extremely supportive, and I appreciate him more than words can express. The journey is at the stage where I clearly see God's plan, and I finally received the breakthrough that I was longing for. I had to toil for it, I waited for it, I humbled myself before the heavenly Father and I now see how obedience and sacrifice pays off with unimaginable rewards. I am an accredited Spanish & French educator, a children's storyteller & writer, a creative director for wedding graphics and more, an author with my second book on the way and a child of God who can do ALL things through Christ who strengthens me!

I wanted to WIN. I had to make SACRIFICES, and above all I had to WAIT. What does that look like? Winning is not a competition or a comparison. It's an independent mentality to maintain your focus, stay in your lane, improve yourself and ninja through the naysayers. Sacrifice means doing something different, being consistent and disciplined, setting goals and smart balancing. Waiting means being patient with yourself while trusting the process, and most importantly, trusting God's timing.

There's more to the testimony, but I'll leave that for another floor. In the meantime – Sit in silence. Pray earnestly. Trust God wholeheartedly. Let your success be your noise and humility your survival tool.

The Final Analogy

Life can be seen as a park; the one where you can clearly see God's spectacular creations – the trees, the carefree birds, the sunshine, a beautiful little lake with ducks, and innocent children frolicking. This represents all the good things in life. This symbolizes life's positive images that make life truly blissful and simply simple. Then in the park there is a man rummaging through the rubbish, a woman sitting alone with a child, boys harshly arguing, an old couple observing, and a daydreamer sprawled on the grass – these are symbolic of life's harsh and unbearable realities. As you walk through the park of life bridled with good, bad and in between. How will you walk?

Heavy burdened?

Confused?

Hopeless?

Frustrated?

Seeking answers?

Yes, yes, and yes. Most times negativity is positivity's unfavourable successor. However, positive energy, positive thinking and positive vibrations are efforts that we all have to put out in order to operate at an optimal level. Negativity can knock you out cold. Don't stay in its coma for too long. Rise up and roar into the richness of hope, boldness, love, empowerment and faith. This is never easy, and it will never be, but make up your mind to make it! Make life work, make life worthwhile, make life pleasant by purging out parasitic pessimism. Make life doable; make life! Just go out there and be viciously determined to make it – Life. Amidst all the unpredictable events and situations, while we can and as much as we can, let's do everything possible to live life to it's fullest – with God as our guide.

What Are You Passionate About?

Do you know what your purpose is?

www.ingramcontent.com/pod-product-compliance
Lightning Source LLC
Chambersburg PA
CBHW042049110726
48006CB00002B/342